A Note to Parents and Teachers

Kids can imagine, kids can laugh and kids can learn to read with this exciting new series of first readers. Each book in the Kids Can Read series has been especially written, illustrated and designed for beginning readers. Humorous, easy-to-read stories, appealing characters, and engaging illustrations make for books that kids will want to read over and over again.

To make selecting a book easy for kids, parents and teachers, the Kids Can Read series offers three levels based on different reading abilities:

Level 1: Kids Can Start to Read

Short stories, simple sentences, easy vocabulary, lots of repetition and visual clues for kids just beginning to read.

Level 2: Kids Can Read with Help

Longer stories, varied sentences, increased vocabulary, some repetition and visual clues for kids who have some reading skills, but may need a little help.

Level 3: Kids Can Read Alone

Longer, more complex stories and sentences, more challenging vocabulary, language play, minimal repetition and visual clues for kids who are reading by themselves.

With the Kids Can Read series, kids can enter a new and exciting world of reading!

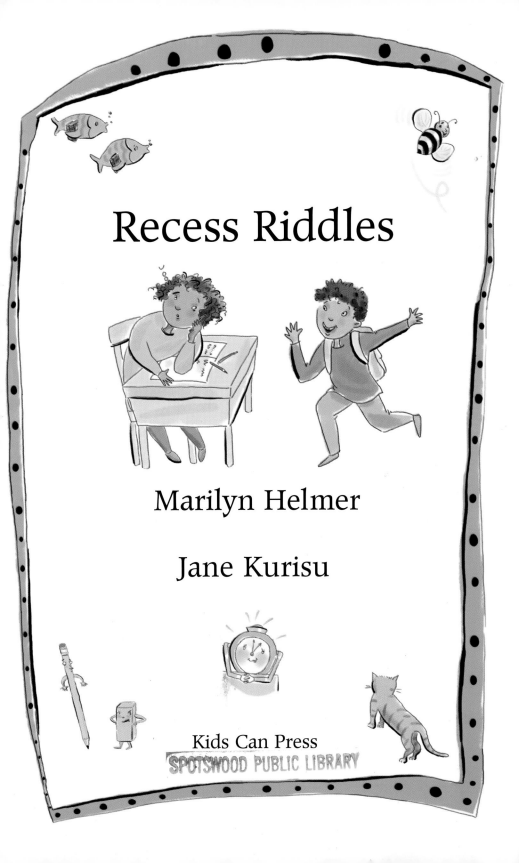

Recess Riddles

Marilyn Helmer

Jane Kurisu

Kids Can Press

Why was the puppy so well-behaved in class?

He wanted to be the Teacher's pet.

Why is the library the tallest part of
the school?

Because it has so many stories

What would you get if you crossed a dictionary with a buzzing insect?

A spelling bee

4

Which day of the week can you chew gum in school?

Chews-day

What kind of bicycle does a gym teacher
ride to school?

An exercise bike

Where do students sit when they are learning math?

At multiplication tables

What was the little snake's best subject in school?

Hiss-story

Why are fish such good students?

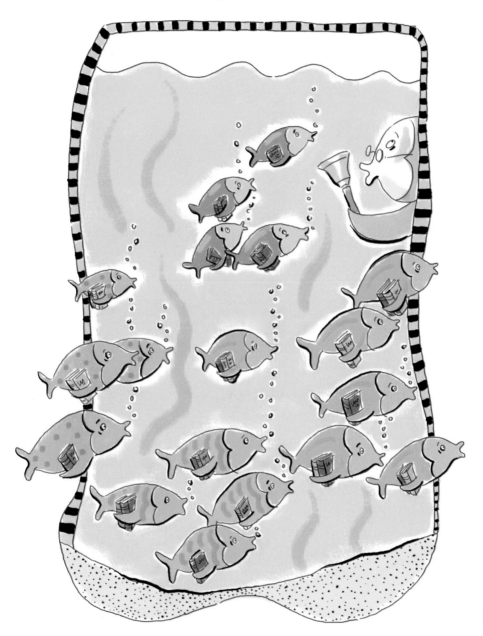

Because they like to hang around in schools

How did the lamb do on his test?

Baa-dly!

Why are principals so friendly?

Because they are princi-pals

What did the Three Little Pigs use to do their homework?

Pen and oink

Why did the clock get into trouble at school?

Because it tocked in class

What do ducks do when they don't know
how to spell a word?

They look it up in the duck-tionary.

Knock, knock.

Who's there?

Teacher.

Teacher who?

Teacher dog not to eat your homework!

15

What did the eraser say to the pencil?

"Don't rub me the wrong way!"

How did the teacher fix her broken ruler?

With measuring tape

What kind of school would you find on top of a mountain?

A high school

When is a report card like a flower garden?

When it's full of Bs

How do bats line up in school?

In alpha-bat-ical order

What did the little skunk like best about school?

Show and Smell

How did the teacher unlock the door to the music room?

With a piano key

What is yellow, has four wheels and lots of arms and legs?

A school bus full of children

How did the giraffe do in school?

She was at the top of her class.

What goes around the schoolyard but
never moves?

A fence

What animal would you find in the school library?

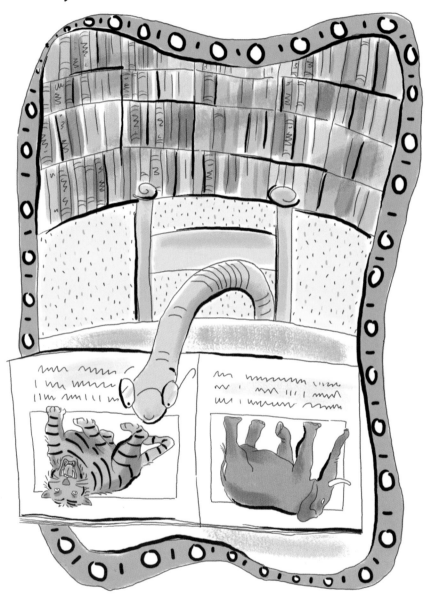

A bookworm

What did Dracula learn in school?

Count-ing

Where do cats go on school trips?

To mew-seums

Why do math teachers like calculators?

Because you can always count on them

Where should you go if you want to be a nurse?

To nurse-ry school

What is the best place to learn about plants?

In kinder-garden

For my daughter, Sandra, now a teacher herself. — M.H.
To Larry. — J.K.

Kids Can Read is a trademark of Kids Can Press

Text © 2004 Marilyn Helmer
Illustrations © 2004 Jane Kurisu

Kids Can Press acknowledges the financial support of the Government of Ontario, through the Ontario Media Development Corporation's Ontario Book Initiative; the Ontario Arts Council; the Canada Council for the Arts; and the Government of Canada, through the BPIDP, for our publishing activity.

Published in Canada by   Published in the U.S. by
Kids Can Press Ltd.   Kids Can Press Ltd.
29 Birch Avenue   2250 Military Road
Toronto, ON M4V 1E2   Tonawanda, NY 14150

www.kidscanpress.com

Edited by David MacDonald
Designed by Stacie Bowes and Marie Bartholomew
Printed in Hong Kong, China, by Wing King Tong

The hardcover edition of this book is smyth sewn casebound.
The paperback edition of this book is limp sewn with a drawn-on cover.

CM 04 0 9 8 7 6 5 4 3 2 1
CM PA 04 0 9 8 7 6 5 4 3 2 1

National Library of Canada Cataloguing in Publication Data

Helmer, Marilyn

    Recess riddles / Marilyn Helmer, Jane Kurisu.

(Kids Can read)
ISBN 1-55337-577-7 (bound).   ISBN 1-55337-578-5 (pbk.)

1. Riddles, Juvenile. I. Kurisu, Jane II. Title. III. Series: Kids Can read (Toronto, Ont.)

PN6371.5.H446 2004   jC818'.5402   C2003-902332-X

Kids Can Press is a *l©rus*™ Entertainment company